Towards Mental Health

The Schizophrenic Problem

LONDON : HUMPHREY MILFORD
OXFORD UNIVERSITY PRESS

TOWARDS MENTAL HEALTH

THE SCHIZOPHRENIC PROBLEM

BY

CHARLES MACFIE CAMPBELL

CAMBRIDGE

HARVARD UNIVERSITY PRESS

MCMXXXIII

PRINTED AT THE HARVARD UNIVERSITY PRESS
CAMBRIDGE, MASS., U. S. A.

Preface

FOR the Adolph Gehrmann lectures in hygiene at the University of Illinois College of Medicine in 1932 the committee in charge chose the topic of mental hygiene. This was the first time since the foundation of the lectureship that the hygiene of the complete individual had been the subject of discussion; previous lecturers had discussed special dangers to the constituent systems of the individual.

In the presentation of the field of mental hygiene it is possible to select simple and striking situations, where preventive work brings obvious gains; a collection of such instances makes the task of mental hygiene appear to be plain sailing. At the present juncture it seems equally desirable to emphasize the complexities of the task of mental hygiene; oversimplification is apt to lead later to disillusionment.

The material for these lectures represents some of the most difficult problems in the field of mental disorders; it is hoped that these difficulties will not discourage but will act as a stimulus and a challenge.

PREFACE

The lectures were prepared for an audience of faculty members, alumni, advanced students and undergraduates interested in this field; although prepared for a medical audience they discuss no clinical detail, but stress the broader aspect of the individual's adaptation to the cultural environment, and may therefore be of interest to non-medical workers in the social field.

C. M. C.

CAMBRIDGE, February, 1933

Contents

Towards Mental Health

The Schizophrenic Problem

I

The General Field and the Special Territory

THE EMPHASIS OF HYGIENE ON IMPERSONAL FACTORS

THE science of hygiene has until recently laid little emphasis on the specific human factor. It has chiefly aimed to preserve the organism from deleterious agents of impersonal nature, and to supply the requisites for the welfare of the constituent tissues and organs of the body. Through its successful accomplishments it has laid every member of a civilized community under its debt for his personal welfare and his security from various dangers. Hygiene on the whole has dealt more with the duration of life than with its quality; it has safeguarded and supported the tissues and organs without concern as to the use made of these organs for the purposes of the individual life. Hygiene has not considered within its sphere the contribution due from the individual to the social group, nor the intangible factors which the individual must obtain from the cultural environment in order to maintain a healthy balance.

A new department of hygiene is rapidly developing which makes these human factors its main concern; it leaves to general hygiene the study of the principles and of the measures which are important for the integrity of the physical machine, but takes for its concern those functions of the organism which give to it its human quality, functions in virtue of which the individual attains a certain internal equilibrium, plays his rôle as a member of the social group and adapts himself to the world in its wider aspects.

It is, therefore, encouraging to find that those who administer the Gehrmann Lectures in Hygiene have seen fit to make the topic of the lectures for this year Mental Hygiene, a department of knowledge with foundations somewhat insecure and boundaries ill-delimited, but dealing with issues of the greatest importance to the individual and to the community.

The general science of hygiene presents to us an organized body of knowledge supported by a formidable array of experimental and statistical evidence dealing with morbidity and mortality; the emphasis is on causal factors, and especially on those causal factors which are open to individual and to social control. One expects in a lecture on hygiene to have definite statements as to the causes of disease, with suggestions as to methods of dealing with these causes and with statistical evidence, if possible, to show that application of these methods has already resulted in definite modification of the morbidity or mortality of the diseases discussed. In the general field of hygiene the diseases discussed are, as a rule, associated with definite tissue reactions or biochemical changes, and have simple and demonstrable causes such as lack of sunshine (e.g. rickets), deficiency of certain essential components in the diet (e.g. scurvy), malnutrition and poor housing conditions (contributory to tuberculosis), poisons in food or drink or atmosphere (e.g. in various occupations), parasitic and microbic agents (e.g. hookworm, malaria, infectious diseases).

In this field many problems can be attacked by methods of great precision, e.g. the analysis of diet (chemical composition, caloric value, vitamine content), the testing of a milk or water supply (chemical and bacteriological analysis), the study of the transmission of disease from individual to individual. It is often possible to reproduce the disease in experimental animals and thus to study it under the controlled conditions of the laboratory, apart from the disturbing variables of human life.

THE IMPORTANCE OF THE PERSONALITY AND OF THE SOCIAL SITUATION IN MENTAL HYGIENE

In the field of mental hygiene the situation is different, and the importance of this difference, not always recognized, requires a brief discussion of certain fundamental principles. In general medicine and in all the special fields of medicine or of surgery one works with the same fundamental concepts, the same impersonal categories, namely those of physics, chemistry, physiology, pathology, immunology. The transition from one specialty to another may require a change of emphasis on tissues and processes involved but introduces no fundamentally new principles; the concept of disease remains the same, and is an impersonal matter connoting certain abnormalities in the processes of nutrition, in the maintenance of the *milieu interne*, in hormonic and neurological integration, in the defense against foreign proteins and organismal irritants.

With the persistence of an earlier mode of thought beneath our present sophisticated beliefs disease is often thought of as an independent entity, almost as substantial as the piece of quartz which the Australian medicine-man seems to extract from the body of his patient and which he demonstrates as the disease. The laboratory-minded physician in his clinical work is apt to look upon the patient as the more or less incidental battleground upon which a fascinating conflict of impersonal forces is taking place. He hopes to find the key to the disorder in some biochemical or physiological anomaly, in the presence of an infective agent or in the evidence supplied eventually by histopathological changes. Failure along these lines to solve the nature of the disease does not make him distrust his method of attack; he hopes that a more refined technique and a more prolonged search will bring the desired solution.

This attitude ignores the possibility that the technical methods which have been so productive in the field of internal medicine may have a strictly limited application in the field of mental disorders. Methods designed for the study of metabolic and infective processes may fail to throw much light on distorted behaviour and beliefs. It is well to realize that the total endowment of the individual and the forces which are involved in the equilibrium of the personality are not capable of formulation in terms so simple as those of the biochemist or the physiologist.

Owing to the disinclination to see in the symptoms of a patient any other factor at work than those studied in the impersonal medical sciences, the medical profession has for long been strikingly inefficient in dealing with many cases of apparent physical invalidism (neuroses), the nature of which became more generally recognized in war-time dress than in the ordinary garb of peace.

The physician who is interested in the field of mental disorders, and in that of human maladjustment in general, must take a broader point of view than is necessary for the study of disease processes; he has to restore the patient to the equation, he has to study anew the human personality, provisionally neglected during an era of startling discoveries in the laboratory.

For a certain group of mental disorders the narrow traditional point of view of general medicine may be more or less adequate; in this group of disorders (organic psychoses, toxic and infective psychoses, symptomatic psychoses) the fundamental disorder is of impersonal nature and has to be studied by the methods of internal medicine; the disturbance of the higher functions, the mental symptoms are to a large extent if not wholly the secondary result of the underlying impersonal disorder.

In many other disorders, however, there is no such evidence of disorder at the level of the simpler functions, and to pin one's hope of an explanation on the further refinement of biochemical or physiological analysis is to ignore a great body of facts which indicate that the explanation is to be found in another direction.

The first task of the investigator is to observe carefully and impartially and not to discard prematurely any of the facts in the situation. In the field of mental disorders it is specially important that the physician should come to his patients with an open and receptive attitude and face the real complexity of the situation; he must not neglect those aspects of it, which do not fit in with the conventional concept of disease, and which do not lend themselves to the methods of precision which have been of value in the study of metabolic and infectious diseases. In the field of mental disorders one has to face the concrete problem of the patient with his incapacity, living in the complicated web of actual circumstances. One has to use whatever methods are suitable in order to study the origin of the morbid behaviour, moods and beliefs. In this study the physician must not only have a good grasp of the methods and facts of internal medicine; he needs insight into human nature and the conditions of human life. He must not discard sound knowledge of human traits and of the complicated structure of human personality merely because these latter are ignored in other branches of medicine and are not topics of physiological investigation. The physiologist does not claim to study man in the fullness of his nature, and in those functions which he does not investigate may lie the key to many a mental disorder.

In the course of these lectures much will be said about the personality and about the life situation, about emotions and attitudes. It may be well here at the beginning to state expressly that, when one talks of the morbid attitude of a patient, one does not ignore his biochemical equilibrium, when one calls attention to the social situation to which a patient had to react, one is not neglecting the histopathological findings in the brain that may be demonstrated after death; in the reaction of the patient to the life situation all the equipment of the individual is mobilized, and in this mobilization the brain, like the thyroid gland and the heart, plays its own special rôle; it may prove unequal to the demand made upon it by the environmental stress even although not damaged by any primary interference with nutrition or by any toxic factors of exogenous origin.

To some, psychological terms such as moods, attitudes, ideas, beliefs seem to be scholastic abstractions, but to the psychiatrist these terms have not become divorced from their complicated setting of human behaviour, which can also be studied at the physiological and at the chemical level.

In discussing the abnormal behaviour or disturbed mood of an individual one wishes to pay attention to any disorder in the physiological field, but one must protest against leaving out of consideration other facts, such as the formation of habits, the moulding influence of the environment, the influence of special emergencies. The laboratory study of a fanatical agnostic may reveal some anomalies in his biochemical equilibrium; to lay the whole weight of the explanation of his agnosticism on such anomalies and to ignore the fact that the agnosticism developed acutely after his wife had run off with a clergyman seems a mistake. To introduce the flight of the wife into an etiological consideration of the attitude of the agnostic does not necessarily indicate an unscientific naïveté nor does it minimize the rôle played in the total reaction by the cerebral cortex, nor should it make the physician less interested in interpreting whatever changes may be found in the agnostic cerebral cortex after death.

In other cases of less simple type it seems equally desirable to study the personality and the total situation in order to understand the patient's change of attitude and of conduct, and in these cases, too, it would stultify any attempt to understand the sequence of events if one were to confine one's attention to the data of the biochemical, the physiological or the histopathological laboratory.

It is true that our agnostic patient might have met his trial more satisfactorily if he had been in more robust physical health, if there had been no focal infection of the teeth and no intestinal stasis and if some polyglandular therapy had supplemented his wavering glands.

A deserted husband may go further than change his creed, he may show a changed attitude towards the values of the immediate social environment, he may show less considerate behaviour, he may shave less frequently and dress less tidily and slide somewhat down the social scale; in regard to the equilibrium between underlying appetites and restraining forces he may be able to mobilize less effort for the conflict, he may take to drink. With this relaxation of effort there may be the emergence of repressed desires, reactivation of discarded indulgences; desire, with no satisfaction from the real world, may call upon the imagination, and the world seen now through the medium of the disturbed personality becomes responsive to the needs of the individual. How far such an individual slides down the social scale, how far his creed becomes distorted, how far primitive tendencies succeed in reasserting themselves, depends upon a complicated group of factors with which physiology as such does not concern itself; it depends upon the complex endowment of the individual and upon the history of the various stages in the development of the individual personality. One can hardly expect that the microscopic changes in the cerebral cortex of the dead agnostic will furnish a complete explanation for the abrupt change in the direction of his career and in the level of his standards.

In the field of mental disorders, whether the interest is in the therapeutic or the preventive aspect, it is clear that we shall have to consider more than physiological and pathological problems, that we shall have to reckon with human nature in its fullness, with the complex organization of its forces at different levels. In considering the individual patient one will not neglect the fundamental processes but will consider the personality as well as the chemical equilibrium, the imagination as well as the digestion, the mental attitude as well as the physical posture, the response to social factors as well as to foreign proteins or pathogenic organisms.

MENTAL DISORDER CONSIDERED AS HUMAN NATURE WORKING UNDER DIFFICULTIES

Mental disorders in the past have been thought of in terms of insanity, a dread disease treated in remote institutions. It is better to define mental disorders as all disorders which require for their formulation reference to the instincts, emotions, thought processes and to the adaptation of the individual to his social environment. The field of mental disorders, therefore, includes not only insanity but hysterical symptoms, morbid fears, compulsive states, much chronic invalidism both medical and surgical, many cases of delinquency and alcoholism, many embittered, thwarted, inhibited, distorted personalities, many individuals with ill-balanced and eccentric views of life.

To free ourselves from the insidious associations of such terms as *disease* and *insanity*, it is well in the field of mental hygiene to keep always in mind that the problem is the prevention of distorted or handicapped lives, with the further goal of promoting in a positive way the full utilization of human endowment. A life distorted by a mental disorder may owe this handicap to a head injury, encephalitis, pellagra, to a great variety of somatic factors, and the promotion of general hygiene with the reduction of metabolic and infectious diseases will be a valuable contribution to the field of mental hygiene. On the other hand, many lives which are handicapped through morbid fears, undue emphasis on physical symptoms, disturbing emotional reactions to certain persons, situations, doctrines, owe their special handicap to definite experiences and situations in the past. Such cases point out the direction of useful preventive work, and it is hoped that the modern child guidance movement will not only help many a child in the period of actual difficulty but will, to a certain extent, immunize the individual against some of the later dangers of life.

Extraordinary accomplishments in the field of physical hygiene have been achieved in comparatively brief periods (hookworm, yellow fever, pellagra, goiter). The worker in a different field of hygiene may feel rather embarrassed by these accomplishments and by the fact that others may look to his branch of work for accomplishments if not of equal magnitude at least equally intelligible and demonstrable. There is, therefore, in presenting the field of mental hygiene the temptation to choose those aspects of the work where the situation is simple and the relationship of cause and effect fairly clear. For purposes of demonstration there may even be a temptation to simplify the situation, and to consider the results anticipated as already achieved. It may be well at the beginning of our discussion of mental hygiene to recognize the full complexity of the problem and to give up any hope of rivalry with the achievements of hygiene in other fields. A comparison of the achievements may be quite out of place, the goals may be quite different. In hygiene in general the emphasis is on the quantity of life; in the field of mental hygiene there is more emphasis on its quality.

THE SCHIZOPHRENIC TERRITORY; THE BEHAVIOUR AND THE IDEAS OF SOME INHABITANTS

The above must be my justification for plunging into a most complicated region of the total field of mental disorders, a region where our knowledge is very fragmentary, where treatment is often looked upon as futile and prevention as utopian. The cases referred to will be, to a large extent, chosen from the field of the schizophrenic disorders. On many of them the label dementia praecox may be found. The term dementia praecox carries with it a certain dogmatic finality, suggests an attitude of therapeutic hopelessness. It is not merely a reaction against this attitude, however, which has led to a change of terminology but rather a doubt as to there being an actual impersonal disease entity which expresses itself in the disturbed conduct and morbid views of the individual. Careful investigation along the lines of internal medicine and in the pathological laboratory has not so far disclosed an impersonal disease process. On the other hand, the careful review of cases has led to greater emphasis on the constitutional mode of reaction of the patient, to the evaluation of symptoms not merely for purposes of classification but for their significance as elements in an adaptive process; the great danger of the patient becoming permanently a social liability is recognized but need not dominate the formulation of the disorder. Expression has been given to this change in point of view by the use of the term schizophrenia (dissociated or split mentality), in which the special lack of harmony or consistency or unity of the patient's behaviour, mood and beliefs is emphasized. In these patients the normal organization of behaviour and thought seems curiously dislocated, and this gives to the behaviour and emotional reactions and beliefs of the patient a certain bizarre and inappropriate quality, to his utterances a strangeness of form and content. With the change in point of view more emphasis is now laid upon the disorder of function as a specific example of individual human nature reacting to a definite social environment, while previously the symptoms were of interest only in so far as they seemed to be useful indicators of an underlying disease process, and were not studied in relation to human nature as a whole but in relation to a physiological-psychological abstraction, useful for work in the laboratory but a rather ghostly travesty of man as he really is.

The term schizophrenia, like all medical substantives, calls up inevitably the idea of a disease with all the associations of this term, and one can hardly escape from a certain influence of the term if used as a substantive. To minimize the tyranny of names I suggest that we should think in geographical rather than in nosological terms, and talk of the schizophrenic territory rather than of schizophrenia. When asked to characterize the inhabitants of this territory we shall admit that some regions of this territory are better explored than others, that there are boundary disputes in certain directions, that the frontier in other directions has not been at all delimited or is still very vaguely charted. A great deal has to be done in the accurate study of the characteristics of the inhabitants in the various regions, or in other words, of the symptomatology of the disorder. It is difficult to make general statements with regard to all the inhabitants of the territory; a statement true of those inhabiting one region may not be valid with regard to those from another district. Many of those found in the territory may prove to be transients. There may be part of the territory which is at the same time under two jurisdictions (as in cases presenting both affective and schizophrenic symptoms).

I shall make no attempt to take up the detailed symptomatology of this heterogeneous group of patients, but shall rather present a few of the inhabitants of this ill-delimited territory. The diagnostician may take exception to the inclusion of some of these patients, but will perhaps be willing to waive his doubts as to their citizenship as we are not at present discussing technical questions of diagnosis but the broad question of the prevention of mental disorder.

Case 1. Agnes B., aged 20, a high school graduate, had been brought up by her father from the age of 7 when her mother died after becoming insane.

The patient was a satisfactory office worker and had many friends. At one period a promising love affair came to an end because the young man was of a different religion. Some months before admission there had been another mild love affair with perhaps some indiscretion. The mental disorder of the patient came on after a minor worry in the office but while she was apparently in very satisfactory physical health. The patient worried over the minor difficulty in the office and was much upset when corrected by the manager. She began to show evidence of emotional turmoil, was restless and talked incoherently. She said that she had talked with God; "the end of the world is coming and we have all got to see things as they are."

In the hospital she showed a condition of considerable overactivity, behaved in a rather impulsive and erratic way. At times she did not talk at all, at other times her utterances were very obscure and fragmentary. The fragments seemed to indicate some preoccupation with questions of personal value: "The signs that point to the wrong way; the finger that pointed at me; I was a twinkling lamb of the Lord and I am not ashamed." Other utterances were still more obscure: "The red automobile was planted in my room and he pushed the baby on the top and he spun round the world; I should have trapped the spirit because I wove wagon wheels round it." The patient sometimes behaved as if she saw imaginary objects and heard voices talking to her.

In this case the syndrome consists of emotional turmoil, impulsive behaviour, fragmentary utterances, preoccupation with personal value; no light was thrown on the disorder by the physical examination.

Case 2. Albert B., a bank clerk, living with his mother, had many men friends and was popular. His brother did not think that he was at all interested in the other sex but, as a matter of fact, he had had occasional sexual intercourse since adolescence. He had, on one occasion, considered marriage seriously but in a rather detached and practical way and without there being very much romance in the situation. At the age of 42 he began to feel that the workers in the bank were against him. His work was probably unsatisfactory, and he was finally discharged on account of a definite irregularity. Soon after this he began to complain of annoyances from neighbors, thought the police were spying on him, felt that there was a general conspiracy to run him down. He changed his residence from time to time. The patient on admission to the hospital talked to the physician quite freely about these troubles and seemed unusually happy and cheerful notwithstanding the nature of his complaints; people had been accusing and hounding him; he heard voices calling him vulgar names; they had threatened to make him feebleminded. He claimed that they were connected with a system of telepathy; they read his every thought and when he went out for a walk the special waves would follow him.

The patient was in very good physical health, the only abnormality being a facial tic, a recurrent frowning and pursing of the lips.

In this case the syndrome consists of a distorted attitude towards the outside world, which in the eyes of the patient is permeated with hostility and criticism.

Case 3. Beatrice C., a laundry worker of 54, rather deaf, deserted by her husband at the age of 35 when she had one child, carried on her simple life for many years with no external evidence of inner discontent. In the late forties or beginning fifties she began to feel that there was hostility in the air and finally she told of her experiences; people had been blowing gas into her room, had looked at her through the transom, tampered with her organs at night, tried to make her a nasty woman, fired chemicals into her, called her vile names. She also made some vague references to temptations against which she had to defend herself.

This is as in the previous case a syndrome in which the outside world appears critical and hostile, but the connection between the aggressive attentions and the unsatisfied romantic cravings of this woman, disillusioned by her married life, is transparent.

Case 4. Caroline D., aged 27, the mother of two children, about one year before coming to the hospital began to be occasionally preoccupied with the thought that her husband might die. She later began to feel that peculiar things were happening in her house. She talked of wanting to marry the doctor who had delivered her three years previously. She felt sure that he also wanted to marry her. Having heard a radio talk about the League of Nations she interpreted it as a personal declaration of the physician and wrote to him: "Dear George: The United States has decided on entering the World Court since everything has been cleared. Please thank all the members. I will do my best to said court. Now down to business matters. I am going to sue you damages for 'stealing' my love story of Nancy and Donald, so tomorrow I am going into town and have myself all 'beautified' at your *expense*. . . ."

The patient felt that her thought was broadcast through some wires that were in her pillow. She felt that God wanted her to help in curing cancer, of which her mother had died. One day she felt that God was using her voice to say this out loud.

The patient had been brought up in a somewhat superstitious atmosphere, she remembered having two distinct premonitions in girlhood. From girlhood she had an impression that she had a mission to carry out, and wanted to become a nun; at 14 she had offered her body to God to use in whatever way He thought best. She entered into married life in complete ignorance of what this involved, and the experience was quite a disillusionment and brought no satisfaction.

Here the syndrome consists in the transformation of the world in the light of the desires of the patient, with startling abeyance of the critical faculty, beliefs of primitive type, loosely constructed formulations.

Case 5. Dora E., aged 34, a stenographer, for some months before admission to the hospital had felt that she was under suspicion. She had been slightly indiscreet in taking flowers from the gardener of the institution where she worked. She felt that the officials suspected her, that they were trailing her and checking her up. She thought that people outside watched her, detectives were after her, minor incidents had a personal reference to her; the special color of the woman physician's dress was to convey a message to her. Some years before the onset of the trouble she had been keeping company with a young man whom she expected to marry, although he had made no formal proposal. She bought herself a diamond ring on the installment plan and told her friends that she had received it from this young man. He finally married another girl and the patient had not disabused the minds of her friends as to the origin of the ring. She had always had this on her mind and may also have been a little uneasy about later advances made to her by other men although her conduct had apparently been quite proper.

Here, too, the syndrome is that of a distorted view of the world, but the motif that dominates this view is not hostility nor the satisfaction of desire but guilt and accusation.

Case 6. Elizabeth F., aged 30, a secretary, had been treated in a somewhat inconsiderate way by her employer and felt keenly a rebuff from him. On the day following this incident she seemed to be distressed, felt that she was unworthy; she looked perplexed, wished to talk the matter over, was preoccupied with a feeling of guilt; two weeks later she retained her urine and faeces, finally refused nourishment. Admitted to hospital the patient was for months extremely uncommunicative, sometimes completely mute; she would smile and shake hands without answering questions, she often smiled and talked to herself, she maintained peculiar attitudes and walked in a very odd way; over long periods she would void urine on the floor.

In her physical condition there was nothing to throw light upon this peculiar behaviour; no gross involvement of the neurological mechanisms was demonstrated, there was no indication of any disturbance of the simple bodily systems.

The patient had a somewhat unusual life history. Her mother had developed a mental disorder when the patient was 9. The patient had been boarded out in a very old-fashioned boarding school and only at 16 had gone back to the family environment in the city to which the family had moved. She found it rather difficult to appreciate the young men whom she met in her new environment; apparently her only love affair had been with a married man. In her own home she had been in contact with a rather unusual situation, as her insane mother had been brought back to live with them, while her father was much interested in another woman.

In this case the outstanding symptoms are the initial emotional distress, with a feeling of guilt and perplexity, later the loss of attention to the simple habits of personal care and absence of any apparent interest in the life of the group.

Case 7. Frances G., aged 38, presented the late stage of a mental condition which had first declared itself at the age of 17. The daughter of an alcoholic father, who later showed cerebral arteriosclerosis, she was a bright scholar but was taken away from high school by her father, although she was eager to continue her education. She is said to have been extremely depressed at this. She took up work in a factory but at the age of 17 or 18 she began to show marked change in her personality. She lost interest in her work, her friends, her music and her religion. At the age of 20 she had to give up her work because she could not keep her attention fixed on it. At that time she would sit and stare into space for hours at a time and would laugh in a silly manner. She would go out for a walk in the middle of the night, at times refused food. She became quite careless in her personal habits; she seemed to hear voices. She was admitted to a state hospital, where her condition remained unchanged for a year. She was taken home and remained there for four years, but was again returned to a state hospital where her condition was essentially the same as on her first admission. She was rather obese, slow, apathetic, with no interest in the surroundings. She heard voices constantly but gave little detail as to what they said. After two years in the hospital the patient was taken home where she remained until the age of 38. During the period at home she was quite childish, inactive, decorated her hair and dress with pieces of cloth and paper. She was self-willed and cross when thwarted. The physical examination of the patient at this time showed a very obese woman (she had been eating excessively) weighing 215 pounds; blood pressure 198/112; there were occasional extra systoles of the heart. Her skin was dry, the hair scanty.

In this case there is an insidious mental and physical deterioration with few indications of emotional turmoil or of distorted beliefs, and with evidence of definite anomalies at the physiological level.

ON THE ADAPTIVE VALUE OF SOME SCHIZO-PHRENIC BEHAVIOUR AND IDEAS

I have presented very brief histories of a few of the inhabitants of the schizophrenic territory, chosen from districts perhaps somewhat remote from each other. When studied from the point of view of internal medicine, of impersonal medicine, medicine of the laboratory categories, one has not *so far* been able to formulate a disease process as the key to unlock the secrets of this group; nor has histopathology, notwithstanding the arduous labors of four decades, furnished any unequivocal data which entitle one to postulate an impersonal disease process. The situation is different from that in regard to pellagra or general paralysis, where, notwithstanding the greatest diversity in the clinical picture, we are entitled to speak of an impersonal disease process, a disturbance of the fundamental tissue reactions which manifests itself not only in certain impersonal symptoms but also modifies and disturbs the higher integrations, the behaviour, the emotional life, the critical judgment, the sensorium and the intellectual processes.

In view of the failure of investigations at the impersonal level to find an explanation for the clinical pictures observed, it seems appropriate to take up anew the life histories of the patients, to consider the material in its totality and without the elimination of the personal factors. It seems justifiable to study afresh the histories of these men and women, adapting themselves not only to the physical environment but to a cultural environment, in which they are steeped from early life and which moulds behaviour, emotion and belief in a most pervasive way. The study of a hysterical case by delicate laboratory methods suitable for investigating impersonal processes may yield a very meagre gain; when one restores the personal factors to the situation and considers the symptoms in the setting of the behaviour of the individual and as part of the reaction to a life situation, the matter may become clear.

The mere question, What is the patient getting out of it? throws a vivid light upon the whole situation and gives a clue to treatment as well as to etiology. Why the hysterical individual should have adopted that method of attaining an end, and how it comes about that certain mechanisms are available to that individual for the purposes of the total personality, may involve a most detailed analysis of the special physiological endowment of the individual. The problem of the hysterical patient cannot be looked upon as completely solved until both sides of the situation have been thoroughly studied, on the one hand the physiological mechanisms with their individual sensitivity, on the other hand the complex forces involved in the personality and the life situation to which the individual has to adapt himself.

As in hysteria, so in clinical material from the schizophrenic territory it may be of value to look upon the problem from the point of view of our general knowledge of human behaviour; to consider the morbid reactions of the patient to the demonstrable difficulties in the life situation, and the special value to the patient of these morbid reactions, may help us to understand the actual sequence of events. What type of individual reacts in this special way, what mechanisms are involved, what internal and external strains elicit the reaction, what rôle is played by adventitious factors such as metabolic and infectious diseases — these are some of the obvious problems for further investigation.

In the light of the considerations discussed above one may review again the cases which have been briefly reported above and discuss their interpretation.

The young office worker of 20 (Case 1), in a period of emotional turmoil apparently related to sentimental affairs, shows a serious disturbance of orderly behaviour and thought and emotional placidity. In the symptoms one sees little adaptive value, no evidence of gain to the patient; the clinical picture suggests a disturbance of equilibrium on account of inner tension beyond the capacity of the patient to assimilate.

The bank clerk of 42 (Case 2) shows no such general disturbance of behaviour, emotional life or thought processes, but the world of his experience has undergone a peculiar metamorphosis, it is penetrated with hostility to and accusations against him.

A similar reaction is that of the laundry worker of 54 (Case 3) who also sees hostility, but this hostility consists essentially of the endeavor of others to tamper with her and to bring into her life elements which she disowns and rejects, but which make an insistent biological appeal.

In the two cases in which the topic of hostility is so prominent, with danger from the outside threatening the patient, it may seem that there is no more of an adaptive process, that there is no more personal gain to the patient than in the first case with its emotional turmoil and general disturbance of behaviour. The case of the laundry woman, however, suggests another interpretation, for although danger threatens her and she appears seriously perturbed by this danger, at least she stoutly maintains that the danger comes from without, that she is not responsible for it, that there is no danger from within, no danger from the turbulent demands of the instinctive life.

To see the responsibility for our difficulties outside and not inside, to put the blame for difficulties on our fellows, to feel that our nature is free from elements which we consider intolerable and degrading, to feel that we have no responsibility for strenuous effort in facing internal problems, such is one type of adaptation to personal problems; it brings in a gain to the patient, a gain for which the patient pays a price in the way of social disability, as the hysterical pays a price in the way of physical disability.

In the married woman of 27 with two children (Case 4), infatuated with her doctor, again one sees the world transformed by the alchemy of thought; the patient lives in a romantic day-dream to which she gives the full value of reality. This situation develops in a woman whose married life brings her little satisfaction either at the crude level of instinctive desire or at the level of romantic attachment, and in her mental disorder she obtains in a special form the satisfaction which real life has denied her. Here we see an open and undisguised adaptation to individual needs; how the critical faculty can abdicate its function and allow the imagination to dominate the situation is a problem.

In the sensitive stenographer of 34 (Case 5), who had received occasional flowers from the gardener, we see the world again transformed but in a somewhat different way, with neither hostility nor romantic satisfaction but with a penetrating quality of accusation.

Here, too, we ask ourselves whether it is not more tolerable for the patient to look upon herself as unjustly accused and suspected of many crimes, than to face certain real underlying factors with regard to which she is extremely sensitive; when she overemphasizes a trifling peccadillo, while she passes over a major fault, she shows a type of compensation met with very frequently in everyday life.

The secretary of 30 (Case 6) becomes absolutely dependent upon those around her for nutrition, for bodily care and cleanliness, and takes no spontaneous part in the social life nor responds to the simplest demands. It is as if she sought, at least temporarily, a complete respite from the responsibilities of adult life, with a return to the complete dependence of the child.

In the woman of 38 (Case 7), who from the age of 17 had shown lack of interest and progressive carelessness in personal habits, there is apparently a permanent establishment of life at a simple dependent level, with adult responsibility completely abandoned; in view of the marked adiposity and other physical symptoms, complex problems arise as to the respective rôles played in the case by a disorder at the physiological level and by a disturbance of the more complex mechanisms of personal adaptation.

These few cases briefly reported may illustrate the human problems within the schizophrenic territory; they are a challenge to medicine, both in its curative and its preventive aspect, and they indicate the complexity of the field of mental hygiene. It is obvious that in this field the rôle of the personality and the rôle of the cultural environment are of great importance. We are now in a position to look in a little more detail at the actual situations which seem to play a part in the development of these serious mental disorders, and to consider how far these factors may be open to individual or to social modification.

II

The Harmonizing of Conflicting Trends, the Achievement of Independence, the Attaining of a Conviction of Personal Value

THOSE interested in the prevention of mental disorders, and in mental hygiene generally, may derive little comfort from a hasty survey of the schizophrenic territory and may turn with more hope in either of two directions. They may take comfort from a survey of the organic and toxic mental disorders and foresee that the preventive work in the general medical field will bring a corresponding gain in the field of mental disorders, reducing the mental casualties from syphilis and alcoholism, from encephalitis and pellagra, from the anemias, the endocrinopathies, cardio-renal-vascular conditions, etc. In the field of the psychoneuroses, too, there may seem room for hope, for in this field the importance of early conditioning factors, of unintelligent repression of the instinctive forces, of undue thwarting or undue exaltation of the expression of individuality, gives practical suggestions for child guidance. It is hoped that the latter will bear fruit in the reduction of those mental disorders, the psychoneuroses, the roots of which lie to a large extent in the early management of the instincts and of the emotional relations of the individual to the group.

The rapid survey of the schizophrenic field shows another picture. In this group of disorders we neither have the clean-cut and simple underlying basis of the organic psychoses nor the fairly obvious mechanisms of the simpler psychoneuroses. Not only is there great difference of opinion in many a case as to its admission to the schizophrenic group, but there is much discussion as to the actual causation of those cases which would unanimously be admitted to the group. Rival schools emphasize the respective importance of hypothetical biochemical, endocrine, bacteriological factors on the one hand, and of hypothetical dynamic psychological factors on the other. We must be grateful for the material of observation which is brought forth in support of both the schools, as the material from both sources may be essential for a complete understanding of these disorders.

Notwithstanding the complexity of the situation

and our present ignorance of many of the factors involved, there may be even now in this field some suggestions for preventive work, some hint for guidance as to the conduct of life. In this hope one returns to survey the clinical material. The clinical material is heterogeneous; there are clinical pictures of great diversity, life histories of infinite variety. We have seen, however, that there are certain types of reaction represented in this diverse material, and much of the diversity may be due to more or less incidental factors in the personal make-up and in the life situation of the individual. One gains the impression that these types of reaction represent the mobilization of the resources of the individual to obtain satisfaction and to establish some sort of equilibrium within the personality and between the personality and the social group with which it is associated. The study of the clinical picture resolves itself into a study of human nature in general and in the particular case, a study of the demands made upon the individual and of the sources from which the individual derives support and satisfaction.

One is struck not only by the recurrence of certain types of reaction but also by the recurrence of certain topics with which the patient is preoccupied. There is a deeper personal significance in the clinical picture of the schizophrenic psychosis than in the meaningless disintegration of the organic psychosis. In every case there seems to be an attempt on the part of the patient to establish some sort of internal equilibrium or to adapt himself to the special conditions of the cultural environment with its deprivation or its exigencies, an attempt at adaptation which may take many eccentric forms. In studying the adaptation of the individual to his environment one meets problems of biochemistry, endocrinology, bacteriology, internal medicine, problems of the constitutional endowment of the individual and of the early moulding influences, problems of the cultural environment and of the actual life situation in face of which the individual breaks down.

I shall choose out of this welter of clinical material one problem which seems related to the subject of these lectures, namely that of the topics which recur so often in the clinical pictures of our patients, topics of fundamental human interest and which may be intimately related to the causation of the disorder.

One topic which insistently recurs is the management of the sexual instinct and of memories dealing with past sexual experiences. Another is the relation of the individual to the parents. A third is the personal value of the individual, either spiritual, ethical or social, his place in the social group and in the general plan of the universe.

CASES TO ILLUSTRATE THE FATE OF REPRESSED SEX FACTORS

The assimilation of the sexual impulse, the bringing of it into harmony with the other urges of human nature, the outward expression of it in forms which are socially acceptable and which do justice both to the vital urges of the individual and the requirements of the cultural situation is a task which makes severe demands on the individual. The severity of the demand may depend partly upon the particular culture in which he is brought up, partly upon the constitutional endowment and the balance between the urgency of the sexual impulse and the strength of the controlling forces. The general pleasure-seeking organic tendencies of the infant become curiously woven into the structure of the nascent sexual impulse, and the sexual impulse becomes subtly entwined with the personal bonds which arise at an early age. The difficulties which are inevitable in view of the constitution of human nature and of the demands of culture may be rendered unnecessarily severe owing to the special influences to which the individual is exposed.

In a review of an unselected series of schizophrenic cases this topic stands out prominently. In some cases the topic is directly referred to, in others it is slightly disguised, again it may be so disguised that there may be difference of opinion as to the exact significance of the symptoms.

In some cases the conflict seems to be in regard to the control of immature or perverse sexual tendencies.

Case 8. Arthur B., aged 34, had been seclusive for one year; he claimed that there was going to be a war between the East and the West, the Mikado was not dead, he himself was mixed up in murder cases; "*they call me a fairy.*"

Case 9. Bernard C., a lad of 17, had at the age of 16 during a mild febrile disorder indicated a feeling of guilt, a grandiose trend, a tendency to project responsibility onto the environment; "why is everybody dying for me?" "I imagined they thought I was spreading a disease," "I thought the doctors wanted to poison me for the benefit of mankind." Nine months after his recovery he again became mentally upset, claimed he was God, a great musician; he masturbated and asked his mother *if people thought him a hermaphrodite.*

Case 10. Charles D., a workman 28 years of age, the only son of a widowed mother, for some time had behaved episodically in a peculiar way; on one occasion he accused his fiancée of immorality and tried to assault her sexually. He said that *he felt forced to stand in front of a man naked* and to get him to do "something he didn't want to do." He exposed himself to the physician examining him; he claimed that the "*fairy smell*" kept him sexually excited. After the patient's recovery he attributed his breakdown to conflict over masturbation and to doubts as to the purity of his fiancée.

Case 11. David E., a man of 25 with an erratic occupational history, had been unable to get work, showed sensitiveness at home, felt there was hostility to him. He made tentative homosexual approaches, and *interpreted looks as homosexual proposals.* He complained that his family was against him, suggested that he was not the son of his supposed mother, perhaps he was an orphan.

Case 12. Ernest F., a man of 38, had as a boy shown nervous symptoms; he was a sleepwalker till 15, had a compulsive ritual in walking. He indulged in masturbation, later lived a promiscuous sex life. After prolonged alcoholism he suddenly began to hear voices *accusing him of homosexuality* (this case would be classified as an alcoholic hallucinosis).

Case 13. Fred G., a Jewish lad of 18, described as a frank, well-balanced boy, had recently been masturbating, and had shown special interest in a book

From Youth to Manhood. He rather acutely developed an emotional condition, claimed that somebody wanted to kill him, that he was not a Jew, his mother was no longer his mother, he heard the voice of Christ, *he must go out to Christ naked* (cf. Case 10).

While masturbation comes up frequently as a topic of rumination, perhaps even more frequently do male patients refer to the topic of homosexuality. In the male there seems to be little conflict over indulgence in heterosexual relations. In female patients the question of heterosexual indulgence is frequently brought up, the phantasies or memories sometimes being associated with feelings of fear or guilt. Here, too, the sexual tendency does not necessarily express itself in direct form, but under a great variety of disguises or symbols.

Case 14. Mrs. Grace H., aged 42, had for some years felt that people were against her. She rather abruptly developed a condition of fear, in which she talked of people going to kill her. She told of the priest having during the service made gross references to her sexual charms; she had seen God once, He told her that he would ruin her (cf. Case 13). As time passed she continued to develop further her ideas of being an object of sexual interest to others and of being tampered with sexually. The patient had married without love, had been sexually frigid; she had been a good housekeeper and mother but had lived a narrow and drab life.

Case 15. Hilda J., a woman of 52 of limited intelligence, had been earning a wage of $10 a week since girlhood, lived an extremely narrow life with little recreation, no romance. In the late forties she began to be much preoccupied at times. At 52 she began to talk of young men persecuting her with a machine through which they said bad words. She claimed that the men were in her room, and that they smoked there.

Case 16. Isabella K., aged 22, whose father and brother had suffered from a mental disorder, developed acutely a condition in which she claimed that she was married (false), said that she was living in a bad house where somebody had a venereal disease, and that some man had been in her room during the night (no data substantiated this). For a considerable time she maintained these ideas; in her behaviour she was careless about exposing herself.

Case 17. Janet L., a single woman of 35, worked as a housekeeper, had a lawsuit over wages, lost her case. Some time after this she complained that her opponent had sent detectives after her, they wanted to accuse her of going with men (she admitted one sexual lapse). She had some bladder trouble, which she attributed to "vibrations" played on her by people in parked automobiles; "it is as if someone was trying to pull the heart out of you." A woman had tried to hypnotize her, made some obscene remarks. For months the patient had annoyed a physician with love letters assuming that he was in love with her (cf. Case 4).

Case 18. Katherine M., a housemaid of 45 working in an institution, living an extremely restricted social life, began to talk of men making love to her; she heard their voices, saw a shape, felt a pressure, had sex relations with someone whose voice called her "wife." At the same time evidence of conflict was seen in her reference to secret service business, spies, jealousy.

Case 19. Louise N., an unmarried woman of 43, at the age of 34 had shown the beginning of mental disorder; she heard voices, talked to a spirit, said that someone was trying to assault her. Some years later she said she was pregnant (false); voices made sexual accusations; she was supposed to be the blessed Virgin. She claimed that her mother was buried alive, was a case of "suspended animation."

Case 20. Mary O., a colored married woman of 35, with four children, became interested in spiritualism, decided to become a medium, a missionary; her behaviour became exuberant, she claimed she was the resurrected Christ, was to be remarried.

Case 21. Nellie P., aged 47, had lived a rather promiscuous life; after leaving her third husband she lived with another man. She became interested in spiritualism, began to talk of a special mission in life, talked about marrying Christ or Mr. A., "who takes Christ's place."

The blend of erotic and religious elements is illustrated by another patient from the borders of the schizophrenic territory.

Case 22. Olive Q., 37 years of age, a self-assertive, argumentative, bright nurse, fell in love rather easily, often prayed for a husband; at the age of 24 under the influence of Bernard Shaw's writings she desired to produce a superman and had an illegitimate child. In the thirties during a difficult economic period she began to study philosophy, felt that she was called by God to the religious life, wanted to become a nun, claimed that everything would be given to her through love. One may mention that when in the continuous tub for treatment she felt that the tub was the womb.

The degree to which crude, immature, and perverse tendencies, romantic longings, religious compensations and sublimations, and the craving for personal value or prestige, enter into the beliefs and phantasies of the patient vary from case to case. (Case 9) Bernard C. not only worries about whether others think him a hermaphrodite, he makes extravagant claims of personal value: "I am God, a great musician, about to be the greatest of the family." (Case 4) Caroline D. lives in the phantasied realization of a romantic attachment, but gives indication neither of crude erotic nor of exalted religious elements.

Case 23. Peter R., an unmarried machinist of 35, had always been bashful, "more like a girl than a boy"; he had recently shown a more aggressive sexual attitude, had kissed a girl visitor and his sister-in-law to the great surprise of the family. He calmly went to a neighbor's apartment and in a matter of fact way made the crudest proposals of perverse sex activity to a married woman. In the hospital he made similar proposals to the nurses; he said that in an obstetrical hospital where he had worked he had been led to believe that the orderlies for therapeutic purposes had sexual relations, normal and perverse, with the patients. A faint tendency to sanctify his beliefs was shown by the claim that the Cardinal was interested in him, and that an early circumcision was an indication of his later rôle.

This patient presents the frankest and most unblushing expression of the influence of the sex factor on behaviour and attitude; he sees the social environment as an open feast of sexual indulgence, similar to the edible opportunities of the child's fairy-tale. The introduction of the Cardinal's patronage is the only indication of the sense of a need for justification. The rôle played by the underlying sex urge in this case may be overemphasized; the patient throughout his life had shown little active sexuality and his sexual advances may have had for their chief source an urge towards self-assertion and a desire to neutralize a feeling of inferiority.

An equal absence of conflict is shown by (Case 4) Caroline D., who basks in the sunshine of her phantasied romance with no evidence of desire to avoid personal responsibility for the situation.

The need for sanctification of sexual desire is shown by (Case 21) Nellie P., who claims that she is to marry Christ or his substitute Mr. A., and by (Case 13) Fred G., who feels that he must go out to Christ naked. In other cases the personal acceptance of the sexual desire is not admitted, the responsibility for the situation is projected on to the outside world; thus (Case 14) Mrs. Grace H. makes others responsible for sexual advances, and in addition sanctifies the situation by identifying the aggressors with the priests, even God himself. (Case 15) Hilda J., a simple soul, does not try to sanctify an admittedly awkward situation, but disguises the nature of the situation and throws all responsibility on a variety of unidentified young men. This procedure is also adopted by (Case 3) Beatrice C., an equally simple soul.

In some cases the underlying sex urge expresses itself directly in conduct, while the patient gives no indication of an ideational elaboration of the topic.

Case 24. Rachel S., 21 years of age, an art student of unaggressive personality, apparently satisfied with superficial social contacts and with a sober family life, begins to show less interest in the usual situations; she wanders out improperly clad; in the hospital she continually tends to undress and expose herself, her utterances refer to undisguised erotic ruminations.

Case 25. Sylvia T., an efficient stenographer of 27, after a long period of obscure physical symptoms, shows an unusual preoccupation with a fellow-worker's behaviour; she ruminates over insanity, makes an unexplained reference to "Holy Father," attempts to go undressed on the street. In the hospital she makes fragmentary references to the bond between her and her father, to the elimination of the mother. She makes impulsive erotic advances to the physician, misinterprets the nurse's behaviour as erotic, thinks that others doubt her virginity; she wets and soils herself.

A question of crucial importance is whether in these cases the sexual topic comes up because it is part of the furniture of the mind and is exposed when the mind is disordered, or whether the sexual topic recurs so frequently because it is a major test of life, over which the patient has come to grief, and in relation to which the patient has not managed to establish an equilibrium which does justice to the individual needs and to the demands of the cultural environment.

CASES TO ILLUSTRATE THE CRAVING FOR AN INDEPENDENT PERSONALITY

The individual has the problem not only of establishing some sort of harmony between the simpler pleasure-seeking tendencies and other more complex opposing tendencies; he has to strike some balance between his rôle as a separate unit or individual and his rôle as one element in a social group. The individual has to pass from the stage of being part of the parent and at first completely dependent on the parent to the stage in which he is completely self-supporting. At first the individual is completely dependent upon the parent for his existence and for his comfort; even at this stage, in addition to the dependence on the parent for physical care and for actual existence, there is a bond at another level, the bond of personal relationship. This latter bond persists even when the period of complete physical dependence is over and it may be an important factor in the structure of the personality. The degree to which this bond influences the personality is partly determined by the constitutional reaction of the individual child and partly by the extent to which the parent cultivates the bond. Some parents can never allow their children to emancipate themselves completely and to live an independent life. James Mill could not allow his son John Stuart Mill, even in the thirties, to exercise his unfettered right to express freely his own opinion upon social and political problems.

Some parents postpone weakening the bond that is involved in physical care and continue its satisfactions to an undue extent. They postpone weaning the child, may bathe and dress him long after it is necessary. They foster the infantilism of the child, and this infantilism may show itself later in the practical conduct of life, in the inability to establish constructive relations with those of the opposite sex leading to marriage, in the inability of the individual to free himself from undesirable limitations in the moral code or philosophy of life or religion in which he has been brought up.

The extent to which a parent may carry such injudicious direction of the child's life is illustrated in the following case:

Case 26. Arthur B., a young man of 27, of limited mentality, but able to go to the 7th grade of school at the age of 11. In his early days he had found that dislike for school tended to bring on nausea and vomiting which was an infallible way of getting home to his mother. The extreme pampering and attention of his mother made the normal adaptation to social life an impossibility. Even when the patient was 25 years of age his mother still cut his finger nails, bathed and dressed him. The father had done little to develop an adult attitude in the case of the patient. When the patient, in the twenties, was heard by his father to utter an oath, the father slapped him as he would slap a little boy. The patient at about the age of 27 began to show odd behaviour, occasionally took to bed without any definite explanation. He now showed irritation at any efforts of his mother to care for him, he stated that his mother was Marie W. instead of Marie B. He could not specify who Marie W. actually was.

In this case it is interesting to see the protest against the mother who has cramped the patient's personality and to notice the denial of her as his actual mother.

In the following case the same topic is illustrated and one finds a similar protest or revolt.

Case 27. Bernard C., aged 17, about six weeks before admission to the hospital had shown a sudden change in appearance and in his general behaviour. Hitherto he had been shy and seclusive, never asserted himself, was always extremely polite and was described as "a little gentleman" with no indication of temper or emotional instability, quite docile at home. He had been looked after with the utmost solicitude by his parents, the father a timid man previously a minister now in business, the mother a domineering personality, a social worker for 20 years. The patient had been subjected to many restrictions by his parents throughout his whole life. He received most of his education from private tutors.

With the onset of the revolt the patient, instead of appearing timid and shy, began to stare his parents straight in the face in a somewhat assertive way. He told the family that he was going to assert himself: "I have always let other people walk over me — to get ahead you've got to fight your way."

He now refused to wash or shave. When asked why he let his beard grow, he said "I feel as though it helps me." He became more assertive and stubborn and the family were afraid to thwart him. He became careless in his personal habits, on one occasion soiled the bed. He became so antagonistic to his parents that he would order them out of the room, saying "I get tired seeing you." He finally ordered his mother out of the house saying that he was afraid he would kill her.

Case 28. Charles D., aged 21, had been brought up by parents who were continually quarreling, and had slept with his indulgent mother until the age of 12. For some years he had shown a poor equilibrium, eccentric conduct. In his mental upset at the age of 21 he forbids his mother to address him with the familiar Du but insists on the formal Ihr. If she urged him to eat he would fling the food at her.

Case 29. Dwight E., an accountant, aged 32, had for at least six months been unable to work. He remained at home brooding a great deal over the topic of sex and of religion. In his morbid condition he expressed the idea that his mother was trying to force him to become a priest and to join a religious order. His mother had, as a matter of fact, recommended the priesthood as a calling to him as to each of her other sons. He felt that his family had tried to give him a drug which would reduce his sex desire and thus help to drive him into the priesthood. After a visit to a genito-urinary specialist who passed some sounds on him after lubricating them with oil, the patient felt that his mother, being anxious to have him enter the priesthood, had urged him to go to this specialist, whose procedure was similar to certain mediaeval procedures of torture, whereby injections of oil were used to sterilize individuals.

The mother was the dominating factor in the household, had brought up her children with a strict discipline, did not allow them to play with the other children in the neighborhood lest they learn bad habits, kept them close to the home. She taught them all household duties so that her sons were able to cook and to help about the house. She tried to direct their lives and to determine their careers; she encouraged them and tried to give them a feeling of superiority. When the patient had a love affair and broke it off, he talked as if his mother had disapproved of the girl, while his mother disclaimed any such attitude. In such a situation it is not easy to say whether there is some truth in the statement of the patient, or whether the bond between the patient and the mother is the internal inhibiting factor which prevents the development of the love affair.

In other cases one finds the bond between parent and child interwoven with sexual associations.

Case 30. Edward F., a clerk of 22, had been brought up by a mother who was the dominant force in the management of the home and in the discipline of the children; between her and the children there was a close bond of affection. Although somewhat oversolicitous, she was not over-expressive in her affection to the children. The mental disorder of the patient began at the age of 22; after a serious attempt at suicide he was brought to the hospital. In his general outlook the feeling of guilt and of being the object of a very important psychological experiment was prominent. He passed into a state in which thoughts of his mother were prominent. While he was lying in the continuous tub, piles of linen suggested to him an embryo and he ruminated over this and over the possibility of his being again an embryo and about to go through the processes of birth and early development. He felt that he had been born again in the tub (cf. Case 22). One of the nurses resembled his mother, she seemed to be pregnant; he thought she was his wife (cf. R. L. S. to his old nurse:

> My second mother, my first wife,
> The angel of my infant life).

He felt that she had been impregnated by him although he could not remember the experience, but then again she seemed to him to be his mother and he was going to be born again.

Case 31. Fred G., a laborer, aged 18, in a somewhat similar way, blends the two relationships together, the relationship of child to parent and the sexual relationship. The patient had been worrying for some time about masturbation. Eight days before the onset of the psychosis he became excited, talked in a somewhat jovial, unbridled and boastful way. He was able to continue work during the following week but did erratic things. After this week he developed a condition of excitement which required treatment in the hospital. In his disordered utterances he talked much of sex, said he would like to be a bull. He talked of religion and especially of St. Mary, wondering whether she is God's mother or God's wife. He asked the physician not to speak to him as if to a little baby, then said that he had once had sex relations when he was a little baby; this sex relation was the act of his birth. In his utterances childhood affection, sexual desire, religious aspiration were blended together; he claimed he had sexual desire for every woman, especially for his mother, he wanted to be very religious, to become a priest so that he should be in closer touch with St. Mary, his mother.

The influence of the behaviour and personality of the parent on the child does much to determine the attitude of the child to the satisfaction of the appetites, to the importance of physical symptoms, to his relative importance in the social group. The attitude of the parent may foster in the individual an overvaluation of his own personality; when others do not share this valuation he may feel hurt and unjustly treated, and may throw the responsibility for this on the hostility or stupidity or jealousy of his comrades. The attitude of the parent has a powerful influence on the direction of the affection of the individual, and may do much to limit the later free mobility of the affection and the choice of a love object. The cases, which have been briefly referred to, give some indication of the way in which these early influences help to form the personal attitude of the individual and become interwoven with the various issues of life.

CASES TO ILLUSTRATE THE LONGING FOR PERSONAL VALUE

The human individual seeks not only to establish some sort of harmony between the warring components of his nature, he seeks not only to free himself from the family group and to win for himself a certain individuality as an independent entity, but he seeks to establish for himself a certain status and to acquire a certain personal value. Where the individual fails to acquire this feeling of personal value, the resultant feeling of failure or of inferiority may lead to reactions of a compensatory nature, to discoloration, distortion and misinterpretation of the outside world.

The status of the individual is in relation to various groups, the family group, the school group, the occupational group, the social group, and there are many topics regarding which the individual's feeling of his comparative status or rating or personal value is important. The individual is sensitive to his personal value in regard to physical strength, skill at games, physical beauty, sexual appeal, sexual potency, intellectual ability, economic, social, racial and religious status. In addition to his acquisition of a tolerable status in regard to the immediate social group, there is a vague striving for a tolerable status with regard to the general background of his experience, a status in regard to those ethical or religious values which he feels have an absolute quality and which transcend the other values of the immediate environment. He seeks to square himself with the unknown powers which are in the background of experience, to attain comfort and security by feeling that he has a certain personal value in the universe based on his ethical or religious standing. The expression of this urge may be stimulated by difficulties and failures in the various fields of human endeavor.

Case 32. George H., aged 17, a somewhat frail lad, much attached to his mother and with musical ambitions, felt that he had a lack of virility and to develop his virility and his appeal to the other sex he practised masturbation. During a period of training in a military camp he developed an acute excitement in which he expressed many odd ideas. He expressed a feeling of great power, he thought he was controlling the power-house at the camp, he felt that by the movement of his hands he could make aeroplanes go faster. He imagined that during masturbation he was bringing children into the world who were strong and healthy. He thought that he was Jesus Christ second, and was going to clean up the world. After a short time he improved, but when out on a visit, during an auto ride, he kept muttering to himself "I am the king, I am the king."

Case 33. Henry J., aged 25, a mother's boy, after graduation from college made an attempt to work away from home, became homesick, returned home. At home he complained of many physical symptoms, but no evidence of any organic disorder was found. He accepted a position which was quite below his previous position and with little chance of advancement. His life so far had shown an inability to attain personal independence and emancipation from the mother. In his occupational contacts as an engineer he had been unable to accept the companionship of rough and inconsiderate people.

After some months at home he began to make claims of very great personal value. He said that he was able to cure heart disease and cancer. He said that he was Jesus Christ; "I should live as a man in order to guide the future destinies of the world." His abnormal desire for prestige seemed to conflict with his dependence on his parents; "the voice within says I must stay here (hospital) until 12 o'clock tonight; at 12 I shall return to my home, to the people *who are supposed to be my parents*."

Case 34. Andrew O., 31 years of age, a distinguished graduate of a reputable university, after receiving his advanced degree showed an inability to adapt himself to any of the minor teaching positions available, or to take up profitably any other form of occupation. Five years after being granted his degree he was in such a disturbed mental state that he was admitted to a mental hospital. Analysis of his case showed that his life program had been seriously influenced by a feeling of inferiority as to his physical and social status. Short of stature, disturbed by the promptings of sex, he had throughout his life carried out a rigid schedule of physical exercise, hoping thereby to develop himself physically and to be better able to control the promptings of sex. Bashful, and unable to make easy contact with the other sex, in his mental disorder he is preoccupied with this topic; "there's a certain rivalry going on between me and my father as to who has the greater sexual potency." During a period of eccentric and uncoöperative behaviour, he gives expression to his grandiose longings: "the entire country was calling me a hero." Poorly equipped for the practical demands of life, and for social success, he had devoted himself with the greatest assiduity to the cultivation of the intellectual functions, putting all his hopes for personal distinction on intellectual success. His mother had fostered his ambitions and reflected the patient's own very high opinion of himself. The patient had developed an attitude of pronounced mental snobbishness, looked down upon his unintellectual parents, accepted their economic support with no expression of indebtedness.

Case 35. James L., an immaculate clerk of 29, keenly interested in church affairs, quite sociable, was rather dominated by his mother and profoundly attached to her. He had a protracted love affair but at the age of 26, on somewhat inadequate grounds, he became jealous and broke off the affair. For the following two years he was unemployed, seemed to be willing to remain at home and be looked after by his mother. At the end of this time came the acute onset of a mental disorder with odd behaviour and many fragmentary delusions. In the mental upheaval one finds the underlying craving for greatness expressing itself in the following voices which he hears: "You are rightful king of Italy, son of God you are, illegal son of Queen Mary, Queen Mary came over last night in a helicopter to look at you."

The personal dissatisfaction and feeling of moral inferiority resulting from inability to deal in a satisfactory way with the sex impulse tend to find compensation in delusions of a religious nature. In some cases the feeling of inferiority is not based upon ethical values but rather upon considerations of physique and of virility; thus (Case 32) George H., the lad of 17, expresses no dissatisfaction with his own ethical quality but with his lack of sex potency, and in his psychosis he gives expression in crude and exaggerated form to his sex ambition.

The desire for high personal value is most frequently expressed in religious terms, no matter what the source of the feeling of inferiority.

Case 36. Kenneth M., a hypochondriacal clerk of 25, deserted as a child by his alcoholic father, brought up in poverty by a devout mother, after leaving the grade school worked in several jobs, was never satisfied. At the age of 25, without any change in his physical health, he became nervous and began to talk in a rather irrational way. He spoke about religion, claimed that God was inside him, he claimed that he himself was God.

Case 37. Lawrence M., a truck driver of 25, a rather jovial, crude, alcoholic, irreligious fellow, without any known precipitating cause claimed that he was about to die, demanded a priest, began to pray incessantly; after this conduct he became overactive, and now claimed that he was Christ, that he had been sent to redeem the world.

The feeling of great personal importance was exemplified in (Case 9) Bernard C.; the patient in his first attack at 16 felt that his suffering had high humanitarian value (the doctors wanted to poison him "for the benefit of mankind"); in the second mental upset at 17 he claimed that he was God, a great musician, able to be the greatest of the family.

Case 38. Michael O., a clerk of 27, previously a student in a seminary, had three attacks of mental disorder. In the first attack at the age of 19 the world suddenly became to him a theatre of great disorder in which the forces of good and evil struggled with each other. In the second attack he identified himself with Christ and at the same time with the democratic nominee for president. In the third attack at the age of 27 he suddenly passed into a condition of religious preoccupation in which he claimed that he was St. Paschal.

Case 39. Nolan P., a gardener of 23, shy with scarcely any friends, confiding only in his younger sister, began to show very erratic and unintelligible behaviour and conversation. After erratic conduct for three months he was admitted to hospital and there he claimed that he might be Christ or St. Peter, that he had a mission and must die for the world.

Case 40. Priscilla H., aged 22, a girl of poor intelligence, low social status and inefficient as a factory worker, had at 19 entered the religious life. In her second year it became apparent that she was mentally abnormal; she was later admitted to hospital, and there she said that she was destined to marry the great ruler of the earth and to become the mother of God.

Case 41. Robert S., a milkman of 26, the youngest of a family of 13, had been so dependent upon his mother that at the age of 19, when his mother died, he was incapacitated for one year. At the age of 25, after some friction at his place of work and perhaps some injustice, he became suspicious, behaved in a queer and unintelligible way, talked in a manner difficult to understand. Although previously not very religious, he stated now that he was "marked" with religion, that he had a mission on earth to do God's will and to be like the saints.

In this case, along with the flattering grandiose ideas, there were many accusations against others for their dishonorable procedures directed against him; by such accusations, which project on to the outside world troubling factors which will intrude into consciousness, the patient disowns any personal responsibility for these factors and pins the responsibility on others. This familiar method of maintaining one's feeling of self-respect or personal value by seeing the disagreeable factors outside instead of inside the personality plays an important rôle in mental disorders. (Case 3) Beatrice C. and (Case 14) Mrs. Grace H. furnish good examples of this type of reaction to disturbing sexual trends.

Case 42. Stuart T., a laborer of 53 shows this accusatory tendency in a very simple setting; backward at school, socially and economically inferior, in later life he began to accuse his sister and others, complaining without foundation that they gave him poor food, that he had been defrauded of a legacy, that they had tried to make him lose his job.

Case 43. Thomas U., aged 42, a graduate of a technical institute, after the war seemed to be somewhat more irritable and moody than before, and showed an inordinate ambition. He wanted to become rich so that he could prevent future wars. During the following ten years he made no attempt to secure positions but studied and lived a very retired life; he did nothing to support himself, made progressively greater demands upon his family and developed a more exalted opinion of his own capacity. He was preoccupied with the idea of grandiose accomplishments, among others with that of devising a plane that could make a transcontinental flight and back without refueling, and a machine into which one could dictate while the machine transformed the dictation into typed manuscript. For some advice given to his brother he demanded an exorbitant sum, and he called on a high executive officer at a university in order to see whether there might be available for him a vacant professorial chair or a position as instructor.

In this case one sees no direct evidence of the influence of the sex instinct, nor any indication of dissatisfaction of the patient with his own ethical value, nor any suggestion of religious longing; the inferiority and the compensatory reactions are on a matter-of-fact level. Economically inferior, dependent on his family, he does not put forth effort in order to get satisfaction from work done; he utilizes the imagination, conjures up pictures of major accomplishments and gives the phantasied goal the value of reality. He deals with his professional and economic problem as (Case 4) Caroline D. deals with her erotic problem.

III

Heredity and Environment

THE desire to be of help to others is one of the springs of human action. It stimulates the therapeutic activity of the practising physician and the research activity of the worker in the laboratory. An eagerness to help may, however, while it stimulates work, cloud the critical judgment and make one see therapeutic results and the beneficial results of preventive measures when a critical examination of the situation fails to corroborate the claims.

Charles Darwin writes "I am inclined to agree with Francis Galton in believing that education and environment produce only a small effect on the mind of anyone, and that most of our qualities are innate." Even those who share this opinion and realize how much of a man's career is determined by his original endowment may still be interested in that "small effect on the mind of anyone" which is attributed to education and environment. After all "a small effect on the mind" may result in the difference between a criminal and a financier, between a prophet and a schizophrenic, between an artist and an invalid. The line between sanity and insanity, between a social asset and a social liability is very thin.

A somewhat disgruntled and self-assertive worker caused a strike which cost many thousands of dollars. A high executive, reviewing the situation, ruefully remarked that he supposed they should have spotted the man earlier and either fired him or promoted him. A little change in the environment, a little more social encouragement might have made this man into a definite social asset instead of a liability from the point of view of the producer.

The conquest of the air is partly due to pioneers whose sanity was questioned by those who preferred to have their feet consistently upon the earth. The daydreams of these pioneers have been the inspiration of a purposeful pursuit, which has been of use even to those who doubted the sanity of the original goal.

The seed may be of very great importance, but the soil upon which it is cast and from which it draws its nourishment has an important influence on the crop. Where the seed is given it is reasonable to concentrate attention on the chemistry of the soil and its tillage, realizing that no effort will produce more than the potentialities of the seed allow, but also that without effort these potentialities may come to naught.

It is, therefore, not necessarily because one is unduly optimistic that one pays so much attention to education and to environment, but because that happens to be the field open to our endeavors.

THE COMPLEX MEASURES REQUIRED IN MENTAL HYGIENE

It is striking how simple the situation is in the field of general medicine, how widespread may be the social and economic loss due to one very simple factor, the presence of the typhoid bacillus, the absence of sufficient iodine in the diet, the presence of the mosquito with the malaria parasite. It is striking what benefit can be obtained by such simple measures as the drainage of territory or the periodic supply of a small dose of iodine to school children. The vaccination of children, the supervision of dairies, the introduction of a pure water supply, bring in major results.

Even in the case of such simple measures as those mentioned, the coöperation of the community is necessary, the social background has to be reckoned with, and the results are not attained merely through the activity of a small group of professional workers. Before the school children receive their iodine not only must the scientific workers have established certain facts with reasonable certainty, but those responsible for the supervision of the children in the school system must have been convinced of these facts. The latter must be of an intelligence level capable of appreciating the data and they must not be held back by any social or religious creed, which would prevent their making application of the facts which they have grasped. There have been objections to the use of chloroform in childbirth on religious grounds. It may be necessary to convince not only certain authorities but even the community at large of the importance of the scientific data in order that the necessary procedures be carried through.

In regard to tuberculosis, where the problem is again one of very great theoretical simplicity in contrast with the problems involved in the field of mental disorders, the practical measures to be taken may reach out in a rather complex way into the economic and the social structure. One may have to control the milk supply, to modify the spitting habits of a freedom-loving community, to overcome a prejudice against night air, to improve housing conditions, to raise the wage level of the workers, to stimulate the conscience of the industrialist. Here one may have to combat ignorance, indifference, conservativism, selfishness, class antagonism. The simplicity of the problem, the ocular evidence of the tubercle bacillus and of the diseased tissues, makes it possible to bring the facts home to the community at large.

In a more complicated and obscure disease but one which, in comparison with mental disease, seems to be a simple problem, namely chronic arthritis, we are told that the causes are: "Heredity. Disproportion of mental or physical load to carrying capacity of the individual: fatigue, worry. Lowered resistance of the individual, from over or under physical or mental exercise, or from bacterial infections. Faulty body mechanics. Disturbances of circulation, vasomotor changes, loss of capillary control. Perhaps dysfunction of sympathetic nervous system. Failure of the patient, from ignorance or indulgence, to practice the art of living and the science of eating. Faulty alimentation, constipation or diarrhoea. Deficiency diets."

It is obvious that to combat this simple disorder one needs to enter deeply into the life of the individual if we are going to deal with such a problem as "the proportion of the mental load to the carrying capacity of the individual."

In the field of mental disorders, where we seldom have a problem as simple as that of the tubercle bacillus and its ravages, the factors involved are obscure and as a rule manifold. Not only has one to consider the simpler disturbing factors studied in internal medicine such as improper diet, exogenous poisons as in certain trade hazards, infectious agents, but one has to take into account other elements in the environment which either make demands upon human nature or the presence of which is required for the health of human nature — factors which call out man's instinctive and emotional reactions and which make demands upon his intellectual and imaginative life.

It may appear overambitious to suggest the possibility of making the environment less dangerous or more propitious or, on the other hand, of strengthening the organism as by inoculation or vaccination to deal with the manifold tasks of the cultural environment. It would seem that with predetermined innate qualities on the one hand and environmental factors of infinite complexity on the other hand one had simply to let people muddle through life as best they can.

It is well not to be paralyzed by the dictum of Darwin as to the innate nature of most of our qualities. Qualities supposed to be innate are sometimes found on examination to be determined by previous experience; the instinctive patterns once so freely referred to are now studied from the point of view of their genesis in the experience of the individual under the subtle moulding influence of the environment. With suitable education a dog may learn to salivate at a musical note. Pavlov tells us that he can develop the education of the dog to such a level that the dog may become neurasthenic; it may even become schizophrenic. Assuming for the moment that such terms are justifiable, the neurasthenia or the schizophrenia of the dog might be falsely attributed to innate qualities or constitutional psychopathic inferiority by one who had not followed in detail the maneuvers of the experimenter.

Watson has shown us how the more primitive reactions of the infant can be conditioned in the laboratory, so that they can be elicited by stimuli of conventional value which at first are quite neutral to the child. The conditioning factors studied under the precise technique of the laboratory can also be seen at work in the nursery, the playground and the schoolroom; some of the conditioning is deliberately carried out in order that the child may later give a standard reaction to topics judged to be of personal or social importance, while much of the conditioning is carried on unwittingly but with the result that the behaviour, the outlook, the code of the child are profoundly influenced by the values of those around, values which often have not been consciously accepted by the adult personnel and which may never have been established on a rational basis. The individual who in adult life seems to have attained complete emancipation, a broad grasp of general information and a satisfying code, may be surprised to find incidentally that the old code and outlook of his childhood have not disappeared without leaving traces; they tend to lie dormant beneath the more sophisticated adult consciousness, sometimes thrusting up shoots above the surface and sometimes breaking through in rather serious and disconcerting form.

The term "innate qualities" is perhaps somewhat ambiguous. The qualities have to be thought of not as rigid patterns of reaction but rather as tendencies, the mature form of which may depend very largely on the circumstances which favor or thwart their growth. Patterns of reaction may become conditioned by environmental stimuli; tendencies may be cultivated or may atrophy. Some tendencies may be more tough and resistant than others.

The whole child guidance movement is directed to a wholesome conditioning of the original patterns of the child's reactions, and to fostering tendencies which are at the same time of individual and of social value, so that other tendencies may either completely atrophy or become so ineffective that they cease to be a disturbing factor in the individual life.

The physician, who reviews in some detail the evolution of the life of a patient which has ended in disaster, may not be altogether content with attributing it to undemonstrated processes of disturbed physiology, or to some latent flaw in the endowment of the individual, which inevitably was bound to frustrate his career. While admitting the importance both of undermining physical disorders and of variations in individual endowment, he may remain sensitive to those forces in the environment, which moulded the innate qualities of the individual in a detrimental way, and he may consider the theoretical possibility of avoiding such a disaster. As to the possibility of translating such theoretical possibilities into an actual social program, he may have few illusions. He may promise no quick returns; he may, however, consider that due weight should be given to these factors in discussing social organization.

The organic growth of the tree is a much slower matter than the erection of a building, it is determined by fundamental biological laws, while the time required for the erection of a building of stone and mortar is to a large extent within individual control and depends upon simple and known factors. Perhaps there may be some buildings of slow growth, closely related to the cultural evolution of a community, which have some of the characteristics of organic development; a cathedral that has taken centuries to build may have to be looked upon as part of the organic growth of the community in a sense which is not applicable to a factory or office building.

The development of physical hygiene may be very much more rapid than that of mental hygiene; it is more easily under the control of individuals and need have comparatively little relationship to the organic evolution of the culture of the community. The development of mental hygiene in some of its aspects is bound to be slow as it is part of the cultural evolution of the community.

THE ATTITUDE OF THE CULTURAL ENVIRONMENT TOWARDS SEX

Case 44. Catherine V., a shy, seclusive teacher, 23 years of age, became somewhat forgetful, and told her sister that she could not teach boys, she would rather teach girls. After the school term she went with her family to the beach but as usual did not bathe, because she regarded the modern bathing-suit as immodest. In the fall she began to express certain odd ideas. She said that the priest had referred to her in public as Mary Magdalene, that he had told her to go out of the confessional. She said that people were trying to make her low. She thought she was going to have a baby. Some one had made her a bad woman. One night, in a condition of great turmoil, she struck at her parents.

Among the utterances of the next few weeks one might quote the following: "I had to be a chorus girl all through it, using my body and my limbs. . . . The men were trying to make me into Cleopatra. . . . They did want me to be Helen of Troy, but they won't be able to do it because I am good. . . . They made me a sort of a common Statue of Liberty. . . . They carved my face, neck and shoulders as you would an immodest woman. They make a naked savage leader out of me."

At the same time the patient referred to religious preoccupations. She said that she was our Lord on the cross: "There were a couple of carpenters at our house and they put nails into me. It isn't fair to make me suffer for all. They made me feel like St. Catherine because stark naked in front of those girls" (nurses).

The patient interpreted the ordinary nursing attention on admission as an attack on her personal purity. She talked as if the nurses treated her as an immoral girl. She said that they were personal. "Fifty nurses were personal with me. It is a matter of life and death. They have broken all sorts of laws. I had to be immoral. I was naked a few times for a whole roomful. Two nurses were familiar and common with me."

I do not wish to go into an elaborate clinical analysis of this case with its detailed symptomatology, its regressive manifestations and interesting symbolism. In summary one may say that the patient presents a familiar type of mental disorder of serious nature. Her bizarre utterances and behaviour render her hopelessly out of touch with the social group, whose language she no longer speaks, whose emotions she no longer shares, whose values she does not indorse. The physical condition of the patient indicated no disorder of the simpler functions.

While the utterances and behaviour of the patient were socially so inappropriate and inferior, from the point of view of the patient they had their own justification; the utterances of the patient expressed this significance in a special idiom or language. Her utterances consisted largely in references to sexual matters, in protests against having sexuality thrust upon her, in assertions of her purity, in rejection of pregnancy. In her utterances and behaviour she affirms the absence in herself of any desires of a sexual nature, but this factor of which she sees no trace in her own consciousness seems to be thrust upon her by external forces. The tendency to behave like a child, a wild woman, a chorus girl, a naked savage leader, a famous courtesan, is something which others are imposing upon her; peculiar feelings with regard to her own body are also referred to the machinations of others, while she sees in herself no instinctive stirrings or repressed desires, which might be somehow or other connected with these bodily feelings.

In brief, the patient finds it intolerable to think that she should experience the crude promptings of desire. Apparently she would lose her self-respect if she admitted the presence of such factors in her nature. She evidently looks upon the sexual instinct and its promptings as something tainted and destructive and not as a privilege and a welcome responsibility. She does not see the sexual instinct as part of human endowment to be frankly accepted and intelligently managed and equally worthy of respect with any other human trait, capable of being woven into a structure of spiritual value.

When she could no longer maintain the repression of the sex tendencies and blind herself to their presence she fell back on a secondary position of defense, admitted the possibility of primitive sex expression, but attributed this possibility to forces external to her personality.

The question of the previous lecture may here again be raised — is the prominence of sexual references more or less incidental, the sexual preoccupations being revealed when some disorder has disturbed the equilibrium, removed inhibitions, stimulated interests otherwise dormant, or are these symptoms more than incidental phenomena in the setting of a disorder essentially of impersonal origin, do they throw light on the actual causation of the disorder?

It is not too naïve to assume that the actual breakdown of this patient was very closely related to her attitude towards sexuality, to her inability to accept simply and frankly fundamental facts of human nature. Is such an inability due to a peculiar "innate quality," in virtue of which the individual resists the promptings of the appetites and of those tendencies towards organic satisfaction, which get blended into the sexual instinct? Such an innate quality or repressive tendency seems to have little biological foundation. One may, on the other hand, scrutinize the past history of the patient to see whether her special attitude towards the promptings of the sexual instinct might not be the result of environmental factors, might not be due to her having been conditioned by the behaviour, the utterances, the silence, the embarrassment of those around her.

The history of the patient would give some justification for this interpretation. There appears to have been silence on the topic of sex as far as the mother was concerned. The mother gave her no instruction on this subject. She knew that at the age of 20 the patient had bought a book on sex. She thought that she had read it, but as to her reaction to it and as to what had prompted her buying the book the mother expressed no curiosity. One can hardly imagine equal indifference on the part of the mother as to her daughter's purchase of a new dress, and as to whether the girl had worn it. The uncle was a priest and the girl had spent some time in religious schools.

It is seldom possible to reconstruct in accurate detail the individual factors which condition a patient's attitude towards sex or other topics. We are far from the precise conditions of the laboratory experiment. We are justified, however, in looking upon the atmosphere of this home as tending to condition in an unfortunate way the attitude of the girl to one of the most fundamental issues of human life, one which is of profound biological significance, one which conflicts most with cultural requirements. It is not desirable to overemphasize one factor in a group of etiological factors and lay all the stress in this case on the environment. The atmosphere of the home was no doubt more favorable than that of many homes in which children seem to thrive. The older sister of the patient grew up in this same atmosphere and apparently throve. The history of the patient may indicate that she was of a particularly sensitive disposition, and thus justify the assumption of a constitutional factor as the basis of the later mental disorder.

The practical question is whether, with the given constitution of the patient, with her special sensitiveness or vulnerability, environmental factors, open to human control, played an essential rôle in the shipwreck of the patient's life. To this patient, with her own special sensitiveness, with perhaps a somewhat atypical sexual constitution, the atmosphere seems to have supplied nothing in this respect that was supporting or strengthening, but on the contrary to have conditioned her to values which were unwholesome and disturbing. In regard to a topic which was particularly difficult for her, perhaps due to constitutional sensitiveness, there was a definite taboo, an absence of information, a code of values which could not be considered as hygienic. Her special needs received no attention. There had been no discussion of her personal attitude towards these problems of life, nor had there apparently been any attempt to cultivate those healthy social contacts with the other sex, which promote a normal maturity.

Case 45. David Y., a physical director of 46, one of a family of six, was normal in boyhood, received a fair education, worked in a factory for a few years and then became devoted to physical culture. He followed this vocation for 14 years as playground director, instructor in gymnasium work and in athletic games. He read a great deal on his special subject. He had no close friends but had many superficial acquaintances and was considered to live at a rather elevated level of idealism. He had never shown any attachment to any girl and little was known about his sexual life. After losing his position at the age of 35 he was unable to secure steady employment, was rather depressed over this and brooded over the financial situation. He became increasingly preoccupied and finally he stated that people on the street were spying on him. On the night before his admission to hospital, while at the theatre, he prayed continuously during the performance. He talked in a vague way about hypnotism, passed into a somewhat mystical condition: he would lie on his back, claiming he was receiving strength from God. He spent a few months in the mental hospital, did not return to his previous level; for the following ten years he lived with his sister, a woman of considerable experience and good judgment. Throughout that period he was liable to do erratic acts, show odd behaviour, express himself in curious ways; he would stand in queer attitudes, carry out callisthenics in an inappropriate setting, stare at people in a disconcerting way, would not wash but apparently took pains to be dirty. He once jumped out of his sister's car and stood at attention beside a car which had a registration plate of the state from the university of which he had graduated.

In this case no physical disorder was demonstrated by the ordinary clinical methods.

His mother had been insane from the age of 36; one might, therefore, attribute the mental disorder of our patient to certain innate qualities, similar to those which had led to the mother's psychosis. There was, however, no indication that the psychosis of the mother was based on a transmittable defect; it had come on after the birth of her sixth child.

On the other hand, the evolution of the patient's character and career seems to show something more than the mere unrolling of certain innate qualities. It seems to show the reaction of the individual to certain definite environmental factors. After a normal boyhood the whole program of his life, with its obsessive emphasis on physical culture, was determined by his attempt to deal with the problem of masturbation, which he took with extraordinary seriousness.

Masturbation is an immature form of sex satisfaction, with its own special drawbacks, which has to be understood and dealt with by the individual in a frank and honest way, with the utilization of the personal resources of the individual and the social resources of the environment. It is a problem of more difficulty to some individuals than to others, in virtue of the innate qualities of their constitution. Even where these innate qualities make the habit a matter of unusual difficulty, the difficulty can as a rule be dealt with in a frank way without any serious distortion of the total personality. Where, however, the values given to this subject by the cultural environment make a major issue of the problem, and where this major issue has to be met with a minimum of information and with a maximum of secrecy and evasiveness, the personal equilibrium of the individual is seriously disturbed, his outlook on life may be distorted, his relations with his fellows may be seriously restricted and impaired. The value which is given to masturbation is conditioned by the environment, by the atmosphere of the home, by the current views of schoolmates, of teachers and of those who mould the code of the growing individual.

As a boy the patient had received no frank information with regard to this topic. He had been brought up in a devout and conventional religious environment. He had tried to neutralize what he considered to be a serious sin and a detrimental procedure by prayer, regular religious exercises and by making a cult out of physical exercise. He felt that owing to his habit he was losing his nerve, energy and strength and that he had to exert all his energy to deal with this problem; to acquire this energy he took up physical training with great eagerness, gave up his work in a factory and finally became a professional playground director and leader of athletics. At the same time that he had endeavored to meet this difficulty by the cultivation of physical fitness, he had called on his intellectual resources for additional assistance, had read books on hypnotism, mental telepathy, spiritualism, and before his final breakdown he had talked in a vague and mystical way about hypnotism. His devotion to his oldest sister, who had brought him up after his mother was removed to a state hospital, and his attitude to the problem of sex, had prevented him from establishing anything more than very superficial relations with women. He had often stated that he would never marry but stay with his sister. Preoccupied with the sex topic, before his first admission to hospital at 36 he had misinterpreted some quite neutral happenings; in the hospital he interpreted the ordinary nursing care on admission as an effort on the part of the attendants to force him back upon his former temptations (cf. Case 43 on admission), and to show his physical perfection he fought with them heroically and valiantly.

One does not wish in the presentation of such a case to make it unduly simple. The factors involved in the constitutional endowment, in the evolution of the personality and in the final precipitating situation form a complex texture into which there enter many strands which are closely interwoven. At the same time it seems justified to emphasize the simple and obvious factors which are open to human control.

The actual onset of the psychosis may seem obscure in the absence of any definite precipitating factor, but here the time element may have to be considered. An emotional strain which lasts for a brief period of an individual's life may be satisfactorily borne and may leave no serious effects, but the same strain when carried on for twenty years may leave the individual seriously handicapped in meeting the various vicissitudes of life. An equilibrium which has been maintained with difficulty over a long period with the help of favorable external circumstances may no longer be maintained in the face of loss of friendship, bereavement, economic failure or professional disappointment.

In this case, as in the previous one, the earlier cultural environment did not furnish those supporting factors of which the patient, in view of his innate qualities, was in special need, while the apparently healthy development of his siblings shows that all the weight must not be laid upon the external factors.

In the case of (Case 34) Andrew O., the intellectual graduate of 31, one sees the same factor playing an important part in the total picture. This case was cited to illustrate the strong urge towards self-expression and distinction; in addition to this element one notes the same titanic effort, as in Case 45, to neutralize the disturbing emotional value associated with masturbation. Galled by this factor, he had throughout his life set up a rigid schedule of exercise; in the words of his brother "he made a hobby out of developing himself physically, he did this with set purpose and tirelessly."

With the prudish school teacher (Case 44) the difficulty seems to be the acceptance in general of the rights of sexual desire in human nature; with the physical director (Case 45) and the intellectual graduate (Case 34) the difficulty lies not in the unwillingness to admit the place of sexuality in life, but in the undue importance attached to masturbation. In other patients the main difficulty is that of assimilating perverse sexual tendencies, which come under a severe cultural taboo. It is little recognized by teachers in schools and colleges how wide-spread the homosexual tendency is, and how frequently the student suffers severe mental distress from this constitutional endowment, in relation to which his teachers show neither insight nor tolerance.

In a great number of cases of mental disorder, in which the sex problem plays a prominent rôle, one has no reason to suspect the presence of subtle undermining physical processes nor to attribute the psychosis to a constitutional flaw, which has its own special evolution irrespective of environmental factors. It seems justifiable to lay stress upon the moral judgment and emotional reactions of parents and teachers, environmental factors which seriously condition the patient's later reactions; these factors, which contribute something, if not everything, to the development of the disorder, are open to human control. In the case of our prudish teacher, given the "innate quality" of a sensitive and seclusive nature, a more wholesome education and a better environment might have produced a "small effect on the mind," might have given her different values for certain fundamental topics, and this small effect might perhaps have made the difference between mental health and mental sickness.

THE INFLUENCE OF THE PARENTS ON THE INDEPENDENCE AND THE PSYCHOSEXUAL DEVELOPMENT OF THE CHILD

The second topic mentioned as recurring in the schizophrenic cases is the relation of child to parent, a factor of great importance in the field of mental hygiene. The parent plays an important rôle in forming the habits of the child in regard to the simplest needs of bodily welfare and of social adaptation, in conditioning the emotional reactions of the child to objects, persons, situations, in developing the attitude of the child in regard to physical complaints, personal importance, social response, ethical values, cultural beliefs. The study of the nervous child and of the nervous adult, and of disorders of conduct in general, shows the complicated ramifications of the influence of the child-parent relationship. The child-guidance movement is to a large extent a parent-guidance movement, as, in many cases, the most important factor open to control is the attitude of the parent. In our cases two features are worthy of comment; in some cases there is an explosive self-assertion in opposition to the parent, in other cases the child-parent relationship is blended with sexual elements. The first feature brings up the problem of the emancipation of the individual or the attainment of an independent personality. It devolves on each one not only to adapt himself to the necessary conditions of social life, but to attain individuality and to make a personal contribution to the life of the group. For the welfare of the group it is well that the individual should cultivate a feeling of solidarity with the social organism, should be able to subordinate his appetites and desires to the needs of the group, should be sufficiently responsive to the beliefs of his fellows to be a harmonious element in the group. Life in the group, however, should mean to the individual more than a mere passive acceptance of the pattern of action of others, and the echoing of their beliefs. It should mean the development of the special assets which the individual has, and a contribution which implies a certain independence. The extent to which an individual develops this healthy independence may be modified by the early training of the individual. The emphasis on conformity, submission, passive adaptation may be too great. The personality may be somewhat crippled by enforced dependence on and submission to parental authority, the influence of which may be continued in the pedagogic domination of the school, in the domination of the code of schoolmates, fellow-workers, and members of the social group. The adult individual, therefore, may fit in easily to the social group with its prejudices, but may not have developed robust habits of independent thought and action, and so may be ill-equipped for dealing with special situations where he is thrown back on his own resources. It is, therefore, important that from an early age the child should be encouraged to deal with situations with a degree of independence, corresponding to his physical and mental maturity.

The method of education should be not to do things for the child, and thus to spare the child effort, nor to smooth unduly the path of the child so that there will be the minimum of hardship and pain. Education should encourage the child to put forth independent effort, to accept hardships which are necessary and pain which cannot always be avoided, so that the child may develop steadily the feeling of responsibility for facing the actual difficulties of life in a direct and robust way, without automatically looking for others to relieve him of effort and discomfort.

Oversolicitude on the part of the parent is usually accompanied by overvaluation of the child, an attitude which is easily transmitted to the latter. This personal overvaluation may be a serious hindrance to a sound social adjustment; the individual may be unable to see in himself the cause of failure in his undertakings or in personal relationships, and attribute to others without due cause an unsympathetic attitude or hostile motives.

Where there has been marked domination by the parent there may be a dangerous accumulation of tension in the child owing to the suppression of individual initiative, with a later revolt as in the case of the lad of 17 who ordered his mother out of the house (Case 27).

The blending of the child-parent relationship with sexual factors is of great importance for the later evolution of the individual. It may interfere with the normal development of those extra-familial sexual attachments which lead to courtship and to marriage, and may interfere with a satisfactory marital relationship. The extent to which sexual factors complicate the child-parent relationship may be due in large measure to the constitutional endowment of the individual, but the attitude of the parent may play an important rôle in the situation; just as the parent may unwittingly, owing to his or her own egoistic strivings, interfere with the development of the individuality of the child, so the parent may, owing to his or her own special sexual equilibrium, do much to develop in the child-parent relationship latent sexual possibilities, with somewhat disturbing consequences for the personality of the child. To develop this topic would mean to outline in detail a very important chapter of child psychology, with regard to which our information at present is somewhat fragmentary, and views are seriously divergent. It is one of the important tasks of mental hygiene to clarify the situation and to establish a sound body of information on the nature and evolution of the sex life. The still further task devolves upon it of considering how this information can be made effective. This would mean the dissemination among parents of sound information about sex, and the endeavor to bring home to parents the rôle of their own attitude towards these issues in moulding the personality of the child. This is a task infinitely more complicated than that of disseminating information with regard to tuberculosis or malaria.

It is not encouraging to find that this subject of the rôle of sex in life receives at present practically no attention in institutions of learning, where the more favored members of the community receive their training preparatory to taking up their industrial, professional, social and civic life. One sees scant reference to it in the program of most religious groups. Academic psychology does not specially emphasize it, the general medical practitioner and the pediatrician know little about it, the school teacher and the social worker may have received little instruction on the topic. If, however, this topic is an important factor in regard to the mental health of the child and of the adult, the problem has to be faced. The relevant information must be accumulated and serious study must be given to the possible methods of bringing home to the community a knowledge of the main facts in this field. It is obvious that in regard to this problem there is no possibility of a simple and rapid campaign. One has to consider the slow modification of the thought of the community on a topic where prejudice is strongly entrenched behind personal, family, racial and religious defenses. On the other hand, the optimist may consider the advance that has already been made in our knowledge in this field, the beginning awareness of educational and health authorities of the importance of the field, the possibility of introducing this body of information into such strategic centers as our colleges and professional schools, and the large corps of workers, medical, pedagogic, social and religious, who are in fairly close contact with the individual homes in the community, and whose daily work brings them into contact with family problems, and who are in a position to advise parents.

THE FEELING OF PERSONAL VALUE

The third topic which seems to have concerned many of our patients and to have presented a serious difficulty is the personal value of the individual, his status in the social environment and in the general scheme of the universe.

A feeling of inferiority is a very disturbing factor, and its wide dissemination makes the "inferiority complex" a familiar subject of conversation. In order not to oversimplify the situation and to keep in mind the complexity of the factors in the individual case one may refer again to Case 34, the highly intellectual graduate, 31 years of age, in whom the habit of masturbation had proved such a disturbing factor and had led to such a strenuous program of physical culture. In the life history of this patient the feeling of inferiority played an important rôle. The patient felt inferior both in regard to physique, in regard to economic and social status, in regard to his race. Under the influence of this irksome feeling of inferiority he had put forth all his efforts to develop his special intellectual endowment, and had become a pundit.

Such a reaction to a certain extent is healthy, and in it one sees a definite gain. A feeling of inferiority may be an incentive to put forth one's best efforts, and perhaps no great accomplishment has ever been attained except under the spur of some such stimulus. On the other hand, the patient himself felt that intellectual superiority by itself was not an adequate attainment. In his high-school period he had incurred some discredit in the eyes of the authorities by tilting at the school motto which laid great stress on scholarship; in a literary production of that period he took the stand that preparation for life was the real function of the school.

The emphasis of the patient on intellectual distinction was fostered not only by his teachers but also at home. His mother, who came from a more cultured family than his father and rather despised the father, took pride in the patient's intellectualism which continued the line of her own family tradition. The worship by the mother of her intellectual son took the form of being his slave and doing everything for him. She made no endeavor to cultivate his independence or his response to the needs and rights of other members of the family. The development by the patient of his intellectual gifts was not considered by the family as a social responsibility on the part of the patient, as the method by which he could best make his contribution to the social group. It was encouraged as a purely individual asset, and as a means of domination and of personal aggrandizement. It was particularly favored by the mother, clinging to the values in her own childhood home and looking forward to the personal distinction which the patient directly and she vicariously would receive from his accomplishments.

There enter into this life history a complicated series of factors, the actual relationship of which to the onset of the mental disorder may be a matter of much discussion. It is, however, a quite reasonable hypothesis that the environmental factors which have been emphasized in the history of the case were partly responsible for the unstable balance of the patient and for the onset of the actual mental disorder.

For the disproportionate extent to which the patient cultivated his intellectual gifts the school and college may have to bear a certain responsibility. In school and college one finds the patient getting much praise for his intellectual accomplishments, while the general development of his character apparently remains outside the sphere of interest of his instructors. Both school and college seem to have encouraged him to lay emphasis on the competitive element, on his comparative rating rather than on the special value of the individual studies for his own personal development, or on the relation of his intellectual accomplishments to his total social responsibility.

The question arises as to how far the feeling of inferiority is to be looked on as an inevitable reaction to obvious handicaps associated with race, stature, economic status, etc. The inferiority is obvious; the factors which make it disturbing and which stimulate the compensatory activity are of interest. The feeling of inferiority may be to a certain extent conditioned by environmental factors. The community may lay great stress upon standardization and conformity, and may visit with rather severe condemnation any failure to come up to the standard. It may also tend to overemphasize any superiority, the display in a marked degree of any special quality. Prominence in regard to any quality, whether the quality be a virtue or a vice, tends to excite in many individuals admiration; even notorious murderers have been known to receive letters of admiration. The desire for prestige and popular admiration tends to stimulate individuals to attain prominence, quite irrespective of the intrinsic value of the quality developed. In institutions of learning it is not rare to find extraordinary emphasis laid upon distinction in athletics; the competitive spirit ranges far afield, and there may be an endeavor to ascertain which student is the most handsome, the most popular, the most homely, the best dressed, or the one most distinguished for any other of a great variety of qualities.

Does the feeling of inferiority find a fertile soil in a highly competitive environment, where a very high premium is awarded to the individual who is outstanding in any one of a variety of qualities, while on the other hand there is little tolerance for individual deviations from the norm of the group?

The general culture of the community is seriously influenced by the modern industrial atmosphere, which is one of very keen competition. The feeling of inferiority in a highly competitive environment may be a spur to unexpected accomplishment, but the gain to the group is sometimes at the expense of the individual. To modify the spirit of competition and the ambition for personal recognition may mean a loss to the group, a gain to the individual.

Certainly in dealing with the individual case it is very often the rôle of the physician to help the patient to accept certain limitations and to abandon his neurotic striving for some form of compensatory distinction. The physician may help the patient to take stock of his actual assets, to realize that he has only been allotted five talents or two talents or even one. The patient may come to accept the attitude that the true measure of success is not the absolute return which he gets from his endowment in the way of prestige or economic or social rating, but the use which he has made of his talents; it is not the final score but the way in which he has played the hand that determines his value. In his estimate of his play the individual does well to consider that he has not been playing a lone hand, but that he has been taking part in a social game. At the same time one has to admit that the personal peace of mind, which removes the neurotic striving of the individual, may deprive the community of a reform movement, a scientific discovery, an industrial triumph, an acquisition of territory. The mental hygiene of the individual and the "progress" of the community may not always be in harmony.

In the case of other patients who are harassed by a feeling of inferiority better mental hygiene would deprive the community of no valuable by-product of the individual's neurotic striving. In these cases one sees no evidence of compensatory effort, but the patient takes refuge in the realm of the imagination and gets satisfaction from the mere phantasy of power, as in the case of the lad of 17 (Case 33), who claimed that he could control the power-house, that he could make aeroplanes go faster, that he was Jesus Christ second, that he was the king, and in the case of the clerk of 27 (Case 35), who claimed to be the rightful king of Italy, the son of Queen Mary. Still more frequent than such secular ambitions is the phantasy of a special religious rôle, a phantasy most frequent in those who have had a feeling of spiritual inferiority, and who, in their endeavor to attain peace of mind, assume a certain kinship to or identity with the divine powers with which their religion has made them familiar.

ON PHILOSOPHIC AND RELIGIOUS BELIEF AS AN AID TO ADAPTATION

In considering what personal and social resources are available to enable the individual to maintain his equilibrium in the face of the actual difficulties of his life, one must take into account the cultural beliefs of the group. Reference has already been made to the feeling of social solidarity, and to the part which may be played in the life of the individual by the feeling that he is not an isolated individual but a member of an organized social group. In the life of this group the cultural beliefs play an important adaptive rôle. These beliefs have been slowly developed throughout the ages as the reaction of humanity to the impact of its environment, and the persistence and continual elaboration of these beliefs may indicate the importance of them in the life of the tribe, the race, the nation.

In his impotence and in his ignorance, man has constructed a picture of the world which is being continually modified in order to make it more adequate to his needs. In order to satisfy the demands of his intellect this picture has to be modified to do justice to the new facts of observation and to the new insight into relations which make up the body of scientific knowledge. At the same time there is constant modification of the picture of the world in order to do justice to other needs of human nature, in virtue of which man sees the world not as a meaningless system of forces, but as a spiritual system permeated with values in relation to which he feels that he is entitled and even forced to take a personal stand.

The demands which the environment makes upon the individual and the tests to which he is exposed may be beyond the possibility of balance by any concrete activity which will modify the situation; a crippling illness such as severe infantile paralysis, grinding poverty either chronic or acute, inescapable fixation in a cultural environment of drab or sordid type, severe disappointment in ambition, the loss of beloved friends, the hostility of other individuals or groups may in some cases make the outlook of the individual apparently inevitably tragic. Yet we know that under the most adverse circumstances it is possible for many an individual, by means of certain cultural beliefs, to adapt himself to his environment, and to carry on with a feeling of satisfaction and of personal value.

Some may look upon these beliefs, because not arrived at by the methods of scientific observation, as invalid, and not to be taken account of in a discussion of health and of problems of treatment and of prevention. The scientist trained in the laboratory, dealing with sequences and relations but not with values, in the face of beliefs which look upon the universe as a system of values, may simply dismiss them as not based upon scientific data. He may, it is true, while allowing them no place in his scientific cosmos, pay personal homage to these beliefs and utilize them in his personal life. On the other hand, he may study these beliefs as an actual fact of the universe, as a function of human beings, a type of reaction which may have its own proper part in the total functioning of the organism. As far back as the history of man goes we find that he has not been content merely to observe and record, but he has been inclined to interpret, and the system of interpretation has played a not unimportant part in the actual history of the group, and in the life of each individual member of the group. To the physician, interested in the mental hygiene of the community and of the individual, religious and philosophic belief is of special interest, in so far as it involves the personal equilibrium of the individual, his subjective and objective well-being, and his relation to the community.

In a more or less homogeneous community with a culture which has not varied rapidly, the familiar beliefs of the group may be easily available to the individual, and in the face of various disconcerting experiences and serious trials the patient by means of these beliefs may be able to maintain his equilibrium and well-being. In an old community with crumbling beliefs or in a new community composed of many groups of different cultural backgrounds the situation is different. The individual may not have woven into his thought any living belief as to the world order and its immanent values, to form the background of his individual experiences and efforts; in fine weather such a belief may appear to be of little importance. Under the stress of circumstances the ordinary mental equipment of the individual may prove inadequate; in his uneasiness or distress he may now go shopping around for a philosophy of life as he does for other commodities, and with his lack of guidance and experience, he may find it difficult to distinguish the genuine from the spurious. It is no wonder that one finds so many individuals coquetting with fantastic creeds, and so many patients clinging to beliefs that have no genuine worth. The cultural beliefs of the community and the way in which they are woven into the personality of the younger generation deserve systematic research in their relation to the mental hygiene of the community.

In considering the possibility of moulding the beliefs of the community and of the individual as a mental hygiene measure one meets the same difficulty which has already been mentioned in relation to modifying the attitude of a community to the problem of sex. A certain philosophic outlook, or religious creed, or ethical code may appear to have hygienic value, and one might like to see this body of beliefs incorporated into the common cultural beliefs of the community. For the acceptance of such a cultural outlook there is required emancipation from older creeds, deeply intertwined with racial and national traits and traditions.

In the endeavor to improve cultural organization there may be a certain danger; in loosening the structure of this organization in order to modify a detrimental factor one may lose some important gain. In regard to marriage, in regard to domestic relations generally, in regard to the ethical and religious beliefs of the community it may not be a simple matter to deal with a single detrimental factor, for each element is organically connected with the whole structure. The principle which guides us in the situation must be that of organic growth or cultural development, and one cannot hope to proceed in the same drastic way as with a new water supply or compulsory vaccination, where one may not need to interfere seriously with the cultural beliefs of the community.

It is important to recognize the general principle that the mental health of the community is organically knit up with its whole cultural evolution, that the problems of mental hygiene cannot be attacked exactly in the same way as the familiar problems of physical hygiene. We cannot expect the same immediate returns from our efforts, nor the same statistical demonstration of their efficacy.

Cultural evolution, however, is not to be considered a blind evolutionary process but one in which conscious direction plays a part, and in this conscious direction the student of mental hygiene has his share, emphasizing the rôle which man's beliefs play in his personal equilibrium and seeking to utilize these beliefs in the interest of the mental health of the individual and of the community.

IV

Summary

IN CONCLUDING these lectures it may be well to review briefly the topics that have been discussed. The health of the individual consists not only in the integrity of those structures and functions that subserve the maintenance and the physical well-being of the organism, but in the harmonious adjustment of the conflicting pleasure-seeking tendencies of the individual, in the attainment of an independent personality, in the balance between the claims of the individual and those of the social organism of which he is an integral part, in the adaptation of the finite individual with his limitations and his trials to the cosmos in whose web he finds himself an infinitesimal node.

A review of the life histories of some of the casualties suggests that fuller knowledge and the social utilization of this knowledge may reduce the likelihood of shipwreck. The establishment of harmony between the conflicting tendencies in human nature may be favored by an improved attitude of the community to the problems of sex; the attainment of an independent personality may be facilitated by fuller knowledge and more appropriate training on the part of parents and teachers; defects in personal endowment need not lead to a distorted personality if full use is made of the personal resources of the individual, and if in the cultural environment the competitive spirit is not unduly emphasized and a generous spirit of tolerance is prevalent. Even in face of unusual blows of fate the personality may remain intact if in the cultural environment there are still alive and effective cultural beliefs to which the individual can have recourse in periods of great stress.

Mental hygiene cannot guarantee the happiness of the individual, which is partly dependent on unknown factors of destiny, but it can do much to foster the full utilization of personal and social resources.

The principles emphasized by mental hygiene have to a large extent been derived from the study of the sick and of the vulnerable; they are, however, of general validity, and will become fully effective in social progress when they become part of the mental equipment of all those who wish to employ fully the resources of their human endowment, and when they become integrated into the general culture of the community.

Bei Fragen zur Produktsicherheit wenden Sie sich bitte an:
If you have any questions regarding product safety,
please contact:

Walter de Gruyter GmbH
Genthiner Straße 13
10785 Berlin
productsafety@degruyterbrill.com